How To Find a Work-At-Home Job in 7 Days

A Practical Guide to Finding The Perfect Home-Based Job.

Joy D. Gurtiza

DEDICATION

*This book is dedicated to
the magnificence in all of us.*

CONTENTS

Chapter 1   **What You Should Know If You Work At Home.**   2
Assess yourself
Facts Of Work-At-Home Employment
Tax Benefits For Work-At-Home Workers

Chapter 2   **Top 10 Work At Home Jobs...........................**   6

Chapter 3   **How To Find A Work-At-Home Job.................**   14
10 Tips to Skyrocket Your Job Search
Work-At-Home Rules

Chapter 4   **Your Cover Letter...**   20
E-mail Cover Letter
What Characterizes an Email Cover Letter
Final Thoughts on Email Cover Letter

Chapter 5   **Your Resume...**   27
Two Type of Resumes
Things Not to Include About Yourself
Things Not to Include About Your History
Important Notes When Sending Your Email Resume
Wrapping it up: Do's and Dont's

Chapter 6   **Your Job Interview & Salary Negotiation........**   39
Key Concepts That Can Make You A Start During
The Job Interview
21st-Century Video Interview
How To Handle a Job Interview Over Skype
Virtual Handshake
Salary Negotiation
Money Talk with Smart Replies

Chapter 7   **The Psychology of Scamming.......................**   48
How Not To Get Scammed Online
Typical Job Scam Examples
Work at Home Jobs To Avoid
Where To Report Scam
What am I doing wrong?

Guide Checklist and Workbook   57

ACKNOWLEDGMENTS

*I wish to thank everyone who never stopped
believing in me.*

CHAPTER 1: **WHAT YOU SHOULD KNOW IF YOU WORK AT HOME**

My husband and I are both working from home. I work as a COO in a Canadian company, and he works as a Chief Programmer in an Australian company. Though we work in different companies of different countries we are 20 steps away from each other. I work in the living room, and he works in his storage room.

If you have traditionally worked in an office, the option to work at home sounds like paradise. Many of us are discovering the benefits of working from home. You can work while staying at home to care of your kids, or continue to work late at night after preparing and sharing dinner with the family. With gas prices at a record high, avoiding a commute is another big plus i; it saves so much time and we can get more work done.

Many times individuals go on their work-from-home search without a clue as to what they are looking for. All they know is they would like to work from home. We all have different reasons for wanting to work at home that range from not having a commute to staying home with our children to having more free time to wanting to change our lives and situations. The list goes on and on, but those reasons can be very different for each person. It ultimately comes down to the individual and what they want. Below you will find some questions to ask yourself to help you decide why and what type of work-at-home job you'd like and what best fits you.

These questions are a big part of starting your search. Once these

are answered you will know what truly is best for you. There will be many choices to choose from and many scams will come along the way, so be very careful. Search wisely, but also stay very open-minded as there are many ways to work from home.

Assess yourself

Knowing what you want from a job is very important in your job search, helping you save time and giving you the edge during interviews. Understanding this important part of your career profile will allow you to "sell" yourself to employers as the right person for the job.

I suggest you start with assessing the things that you want to do for work, then follow up with the things that you can do or provide for the employer. So, if you enjoy administrative tasks and your skills and experiences are appropriate for the job, then apply as a virtual administrative assistant (VA) or virtual secretary; do not apply as web designer or programmer. It's the same thing as applying for a position as a driver or a cook when you do not know how to drive or cook. (That's silly, but so far you get the idea.)

Start assessing yourself by answering the following questions:

What can you do, and what are you good at?

What do you want to do?

What kind of people do you want to work with?

Why would you like to do this type of job, and what exactly are you striving for?

Write down things you think you are better qualified to do than other people. This can include extra curricular activities or special training.

Write down any particular things that are important to you, and things that you "won't budge from."

> **Note:** Essential to job and career satisfaction, especially if you are going to work at home, is matching your own unique talents, skills, interests, and personality to those job-related tasks and activities that you find most enjoyable, interesting, and challenging to do.
>
> By performing a self-assessment, you'll most likely have the opportunity for the first time in your career to choose the work-from-home position and organization that is personally fulfilling as well as financially rewarding.

Facts Of Work-At-Home Employment

1. Enhancing Flexibility

Working at home may allow you to organize your work schedule to accommodate your needs. Working flexible hours can have a positive impact on work and family life. It can also make it easier to work when you are most productive and rest when necessary.

2. Reducing Costs

You may find you save time and money by working at home by not having to prepare or buy lunches, paying fares, gas and buying dress clothes.

3. Increasing Productivity

Working at home can help you work more effectively and feel happier about your work.

I read that when employees have more time to be with their families or to do things for themselves, they're happier people. Happier people are less stressed out and are less likely to make mistakes. Happier people are more productive, which leads to more work done and more money saved.

Tax Benefits For Work-At-Home Workers

Employees who do most of their work from home may claim income tax deductions for using a portion of their home as a workplace. The Income Tax Act is very complex and each teleworking arrangement is unique. Consult your accountant or lawyer about how this information applies to you.

CHAPTER 2: **TOP 10**
WORK-AT-HOME JOBS

Here are the types of work-at-home jobs for which companies typically hire.

1. **Customer Service Agent**

J. Crew, 1-800-flowers, Virgin Atlantic and Walgreens are among the companies that outsource their customer service calls to U.S.-based virtual agents.

You must have a pleasant voice and strong customer service skills, high-speed Internet access, a computer, a landline, and a quiet place to work—all of which you pay for on your own.

Pay is typically between $8 and $15 an hour, depending on your experience, call volume and accounts. Be ready to work a minimum of 20 hours per week.

Just about every company has different needs based on location, hours, clients, payment schedules, skills, knowledge, etc., so be sure to check with a few of them to determine the best match for you. Some pay hourly wages, while others require that you incorporate in order to work for them.

You can also check these companies:

- AlpineAccess.com - Virtual call center provider using home-based customer service agents. They charge $45 for a required background check.

- Arise.com - Answer calls, e-mail and chat requests for global companies at home. (Some users have reported a $13 background check fee, a $99 assessment test fee and other charges.)

- ConvergysWorkatHome.com - Be a home agent providing customer care, human resources and billing services.

- West.com - Be an "at-home-agent," with duties including obtaining, entering and verifying customer information, answering questions, resolving issues, explaining sales features or offering additional products or services.

2. Technical Support Agent

If you are an experienced information technology professional and you enjoy problem-solving and providing customer service, you may be able to work from home providing tech support via phone/ online to customers nationwide.

As an independent contractor or employee (this varies per company), you'd work from your own home office, set your own hours.

ComputerAssistant.com, GeeksOnTime.com, PlumChoice.com, SupportFreaks.com are some of the companies to check out.

3. Telemarketing

Many companies and organizations outsource their

cold-calling campaigns to third parties. Those third parties hire full-time and temporary workers—many of whom work from home—to place those calls with specific goals in mind.

You may be required to encourage contacts to book a scheduled visit, commit to making a donation, or agree to try a product or service. Your calls could also be centered on debt collection.

Typically you'll receive an hourly base pay, plus performance-based commission. While some training is provided, applicants are expected to have some high-quality customer service and/or cold calling experience.

Among the companies to explore: Intrep.com, and West.com. Take note that the employer should give you the leads. Do not pay for leads; you should be able to find employers that are hiring without paying a middleman for access to that information.

4. **Writer or Editor**
Several Web sites pay for articles, but unless they're commissioning your original work, you simply won't make big bucks. Associatedcontent.com pays around $10 per approved/published piece. Helium.com is another option that rewards prolific writers, and both sites are a good way to build an online portfolio of published work while making some money simultaneously.

Myessays.com allows essay writers to sell their original work starting at $10 for a short paper, and up to more than $100 for comprehensive work. Writerfind.com lists a range of freelance opportunities for experienced writers to pursue on their own.

Pay varies depending on your experience. Beginners might have to accept free products or press passes for their work. Experienced writers can expect to make anywhere from fifty cents to $2 per word. For multiple articles, you might settle on a flat rate.

Submit an application for freelance work on sites such as Cyberedit.com, which hires professional writers for a variety of projects including resume writing and document proofing. Editfast.com also hires experienced editors, writers and proofreaders.

5. **Translator**
If you are a native speaker of a foreign language, then becoming a freelance translator could be a great opportunity. Several companies need documentation translated for international partners and hire freelance translators through companies like Welocalize,
Language Translation, Inc., Accurapid.com, Telelanguage.com, Sdl.com.

A lot of companies require applicants to take a written test and sign a non-disclosure agreement. Precision and accuracy is crucial. Companies who hire freelance translators prefer candidates who are native speakers of the target language, have experience with
professional documents, software or multimedia translations, and are members of a professional translation association.

The most in-demand services include translation

from English to Japanese, Spanish, French, German, Russian and Italian.

6. **Virtual Assistant**

In many cases small business owners and mid- to executive-level professionals require a personal assistant, but cannot afford to hire one on a full-time basis or simply don't have the space in their offices. Therefore, they hire people from remote locations to do their administrative work for them. Typically, virtual assistants can handle administrative duties, correspondence, and other support services that can be done remotely via e-mail and phone.

Check out virtualassistantjobs.com and teamdoubleclick.com.

The International Virtual Assistants Association may be a valuable resource.

7. **Medical Coding and Transcription**

Medical coding and transcription can't always be performed at home, especially with strict privacy policies and guidelines. Having said that, there are many companies that hire home-based workers with the skills and experience to provide both services.

Keep in mind, however, that it's very difficult for entry-level, inexperienced candidates to get hired to perform such work from home.

In most cases, in addition to the proper training, you must have your own computer, high-speed Internet access, and where applicable, headphones and a foot pedal.

Some companies also require you to have your own software; others will supply it. You can check out the opportunities with Medquist.com, Healthiva.com, and Precysesolutions.com.

8. **Transcribe Audio to Text**
Speeches, lectures, television and radio programs and interviews must be converted to text that's delivered in a timely and accurate   way. If you possess exceptional English language and grammar skills and you're an experienced typist with a speed of at least 75 words per minute, you could possibly transcribe audio to text. Some businesses might require you to take a test before offering   you opportunities to work.

Most assignments are handled on a freelance basis. Sites to explore   include ProductionTranscripts.com, TigerFish.com and AliceDarling.com. Find others by searching on the internet.

9. **Mystery Shopping**
Get paid to shop and eat at great restaurants, and then report back to the corporate headquarters on the level of service and cleanliness that can help increase the experience for future   customers. There are opportunities to earn small amounts of moneyand get free products and services every now and then,
depending on where you live.

While usually there are some people who've managed to earn their living at this, I don't recommend that you depend upon it to pay the bills, especially because assignments can be irregular.

Avoid getting hooked into paying $25 to $100 to become an "official" mystery shopper, assuming you'll automatically get   hired. A legitimate opportunity should not cost you any money. It should give you the chance based on your profile, interests and background. One helpful resource in learning more about the industry and finding links to opportunities is Mysteryshop.org.

10. **Blogger**

Blogging and media sharing on the Internet are sizzling right   now, with absolutely no indication of diminishing any time soon. Web sites with videos, personal content and gossip are raking in advertising dollars with each click of the mouse.

You can be a professional blogger, too. Web sites such as flixya.com enable you to post video and photographs and then receive a percentage of the site's revenue which is generated from advertising associated with page views and clicks to the content posted by you. The harder you work to promote your own videos and photos, the more money you'll earn.

Another way to make money is to create your very own blog at Blogger.com. Set up your own page and create captivating content to lure readers to your stuff.

Then add the site's AdSense feature, which allows advertisements to be included on the page. Whenever a viewer clicks through on the advertisement on your blog page—cha-ching! Keep

in mind this only works if you're committed to creating a blog that others would
find fascinating, and you hustle to attract readers to build a following for yourself.

Note: These are the most common work-at-home jobs you can find on the internet. When searching, keep in mind that jobs that promise you armloads of money with little investment of time and no experience aren't legitimate. Legitimate work-from-home jobs are going to require that you have skills relevant to the position.

Many jobs require skills like writing, graphic design, programming or web design, for example. If you don't have any experience in the field(s) you are interested in, it's going to be difficult to find an employer willing to hire you. Most employers who are willing to hire someone to work from home want workers who can work independently and get the job done with little guidance.

Finally, please take the time to carefully research every job lead you find and every site you visit. Even sites that claim to be self-sufficient sometimes aren't.

CHAPTER 3: **HOW TO FIND A WORK-AT-HOME JOB**

Finding work-from-home employment isn't easy. Even with all the online advertising you see, there aren't that many legitimate work-from-home jobs. In fact, there are more scams than real work-from-home opportunities. Keep this in mind: *Getting a legitimate work at home job is tougher than finding a traditional job.*

You could get lucky putting your resume on the Internet and waiting for an employer to contact you. It does happen. But being passive on the Internet is often about as effective as using other passive job search methods, which is not very effective at all.

Keep in mind that the skills needed for home employment are similar to those needed for working in an office. You need both the experience and the skills necessary to do the job. Some of the things that you will need are phone subscription to call US or other parts of the world, computer, printer, software, and other basic office equipment.

You can do far more on the Internet than simply posting your resume in one or more resume databases, but here are some points to use in preparing.

10 Tips To Skyrocket Your Job Search.

1. Maximize online job boards and job search engines. The top job boards like CareerBuilder.com and Monster.com are filled with thousands of work-from-home opportunities. SimplyHired.com, Linkup.com and Indeed.com are job search engine sites that allow users to search the major job sites, company sites, associations and other online job sites by keyword and location. Search using "telecommute" or "telecommutin" as a keyword to find work-from-home job listings. Be specific.

You can also promote your own skills and abilities on web sites such as Fiverr.com and Guru.com to enable employers to find you. Craigslist.com and Backpage.com are two sites that post local listings for a wide range of freelance opportunities.

Web sites devoted to posting part-time and consulting gigs are Elance.com, sologig.com, clicknwork.com, ether.com. Some of them allow you to post a free profile about yourself and your skills and services.

2. Focus your job search. List the positions or job responsibilities you want to perform. If you have a specific company you want to apply to first, write it down. This will help you focus your job search.

3. Create a targeted resume and cover letter that is ready to send. With regards to the type of employment you're looking for, you may also need a neatly polished resume and cover letter to send out to prospective employers.

Take time to write targeted resumes and cover letters that specifically link your qualifications to the hiring criteria for the jobs you are applying for. The hiring manager will be able to see at a glance why and how you are qualified for the job. You'll have a much better chance of getting an interview than if you send a generic letter and resume.

Track where you've applied. Many of the exact same positions are listed on multiple sites, so be sure not to duplicate your time and effort.

4. Build your brand. Create profiles on LinkedIn, Facebook, and VisualCV. A strong personal brand that portrays you in a professional light will provide recruiters, employers, and contacts with a strong positive impression of you as a candidate they should be interested in.

5. Connect with your contacts. Now that you've created profiles on networking sites, use them. Connect with everyone you know because you never know which contact may be able to help you with your job search or put you in touch with someone who can.

6. Win the interview. Research the company before you go for the interview, dress appropriately, practice answering and asking interview questions, and make a concerted effort to impress the interviewer with your skills, experience, confidence, and expertise.

7. Follow up. It's important to follow up after an interview by thanking everyone with whom you met. Also reiterate your interest in the position and remind the hiring manager why you're an excellent candidate for the job.

8. Be flexible. Overall flexibility is one key to successfully working from home. If you are willing to consider freelance or contract employment or willing to combine a couple of part-time positions, you'll have a greater chance of success in finding opportunities that are legitimate.

9. Keep your expectations reasonable. The people who have the most success on the Internet are those who best understand its limitations. For example, those with technical skills that are in short supply will have more employers looking for these skills and more success on the Internet. Keep in mind that many listed jobs are already filled by the time you see them and that thousands may apply to those that sound particularly attractive.

10. Don't get ripped off online. Because the Internet has few regulations, crooks use it as a way to take money from trusting souls. Remember that anyone can set up a site, even if the person does not provide a legitimate service. So be careful before you pay money for anything on the Internet. A general rule is that if it sounds too good to be true, it probably is. For example, if a site "guarantees" that it will find you a job or charges high fees, I recommend that you look elsewhere.

Work At Home Rules
When people think about working from home, many imagine sleeping in late, lounging around in their pajamas and long leisurely lunches. But what people need to realize is that even though working from home offers a great amount of flexibility, it is still a professional job and it needs to be treated as such.

Individuals need to learn best work-at-home practices, like setting office hours, having a dedicated office space, avoiding home-bound distractions, and actually dressing as if you were going to an office. This will help keep your mindset sharp and focused.

As a home-based employee you don't have the luxury of co-workers sitting right next to you, so you'll often have to figure out issues for yourself. If you're the type of person who prefers a lot of guidance or is easily distracted, working at home may not be an ideal situation for you.

Before starting on any kind of work from home, bear in mind a couple of fundamental rules:

a. Keep a schedule. There is absolutely no manager watching the clock to see whether you report for duty at the designated hour. You're the boss, and that means you carry the responsibility of getting to your workstation on time.

Create a realistic schedule every week, and do what it takes to stick to it. This includes building in breaks for lunch, personal calls, e-mails, and other brief timeouts from your work just as you'd have in a traditional office setting.

b. Create a dedicated work space. Your dinning room table shouldn't double as your office. Pick a quiet space where you can work uninterrupted. It's important to have an area to look   forward to working in each day—no dreary corners—and a place that you can leave behind at the end of your shift.

c. Measure your progress and success. Determine in advance the goals you're aiming for, and then work to achieve them. Be willing to re-evaluate your expectations if necessary to adjust for the realities of your home-based opportunities.

Don't give up. Even though we all crave overnight success and instant gratification, there's no such thing as an easy way to make tons of money with minimal effort. Everything takes work.

CHAPTER 4: **YOUR COVER LETTER**

Part of my present work is getting new employees and freelance   workers to outsource some company projects. My favorite job directory site is Craigslist.org, mainly because counting from experience most of talented and skilled workers are coming from that site.

Typically, I get at least 100 responses in 48 hours, depending on the position I advertised, of course. But most applications I receive go straight to the trash folder as a result of few simple mistakes. When applying, do not just apply. Apply well. Write a cover e-mail that addresses the position. Do not just attach your resume.

Every job seeker must have a cover letter. There are virtually no exceptions to this rule, unless a particular company or recruiter has instructed you to forward just a resume without a cover letter. (This rarely happens.)

There is no doubt that a great cover letter can make the difference in whether you get noticed or passed over. A great cover letter can be a powerful marketing tool; it positions you above the competition, sells your qualifications and your successes, demonstrates your knowledge, experience, and expertise. It creates excitement, enthusiasm, and action (and thus, an interview).

E-mail Cover Letter

When you write an e-mail cover letter, you are generally writing in response to a specific advertisement on the Internet or in a print publication, in which you've been instructed to respond via e-mail. Just as with other ad response letters, you should present your experience as it pertains to each and every one of the requirements outlined in the advertisement.

E-mail cover letters are more brief than traditional printed letters. No one wants to read a lengthy e-mail message, so keep your letters short and on target. Your challenge is to write a letter that meets all of the criteria—defining who you are, highlighting your achievements and qualifications, clearly communicating your value, identifying the type of position you are seeking, and asking for an interview. The only issue is that you need to accomplish this in less space and with fewer words than you would use if you were printing and mailing your letter.

What characterizes an email cover letter?

- Brevity
- To-the-point style and tone
- Written in brief paragraphs or a bullet-style format
- Generally written in response to a specific advertisement or online posting

To make your e-mail cover letter most effective, follow these simple suggestions:

1. *Your resume cover letter must answer the employers needs and to uncover their needs, you must read the job posting carefully.* Explain to them quickly the best way to meet the needs they have listed. Use examples wherever possible. Take a look at these two different letters....

Letter #1

Hi Nick,

OK, I admit. I saw your posting just now for the Operations Manager (Telecommute) for Call Center on CraigsList.org, and I'm salivating. I can't tell you how much happy and excited I am when I learned that I can finally work on my pajamas. Let me tell you 3 reasons you should consider me for this position :

   c. **Strong leadership skills.** Your ad said you were looking for someone who has strong leadership skills. I have proven ability to manage and motivate a team, I attached the list of the projects I successfully lead.

   d. **Good communication and writing skills.** In my former job in one of the biggest BPO here in my country, I regularly led meetings to my team. Several times a year, I would speak for my company at sometimes to audiences of several hundred people. I know how to craft a good press release and have successfully managed to get several articles into print.

I love experiences - I completely relate to your philosophy that life is about experiences. I love to travel. I've never been air diving, but it is on my top ten list of things to do next year.

This is an opportunity where I know I can make a difference, and with my experience at conceiving plans and putting projects into motion, I'm sure I could impact you very quickly without spending too much time in the starting gate. I would love to talk to you in Skype. My Skype ID is *joygurtiza246* I'm usually available around 7am - 12nn EST.

Looking forward speaking with you soon.

Thanks,
Joy Gurtiza

****
My resume is pasted below in text format, and I have attached a Word copy if you prefer to download it.

Letter # 2

Dear Sir/Madam:

Please accept this letter and resume for the Product Marketing Manager position as referenced on Craigslist.com.

As a recent MBA graduate, I believe that I offer the skills that are crucial to this position. My background in marketing, as well as my formal education in business and marketing from the XYZ University will serve as a complement to your firm.

After doing some extensive research I am sure that my work history and educational background will greatly benefit the future endeavors of your organization. My work history coupled with my education in business administration has provided me with an invaluable sense of communication and negotiation, as well as quantitative analytical skills.

From both my professional and personal experiences, I have developed an enthusiastic, entrepreneurial, and disciplined work ethic. I possess the ability to work under pressure and rapidly adapt to changing work conditions. I excel in both individual and team driven environments. With this in mind, I am confident that my employment background, eagerness to learn, and genuine character will prove to be an asset to your company.

I look forward to discussing employment opportunities with you in the near future. I am available for an interview at your earliest convenience.

Thank you in advance for your consideration.

Best,
Jane Doe

Now, which one do you think is nice to read and would probably get a response from the employer?

2. *Be Clear and Concise.* Make use of the exact same language to describe your achievements, as you would to your mother. For example...

> *"My work history coupled with my education in business*
> *administration has provided me with an invaluable sense of*
> *communication and negotiation, as well as quantitative*
> *analytical skills."*

YAWN... - This means nothing to the employer. Compare it to this...

> *"I have only really had one job. It was at ABC company near*
> *my college. We were burning off customers to Axcel Inc. so I*
> *helped convince my superiors to offer a great deal of service*
> *to our customers. I made up a business model of our projected sales, and showed how this would improve our*
> *bottom line. My employer agreed, and tasked me with spreading the word. I made flyers and put up posters around*
> *campus to advertise our new service. Our subscription model*
> *was a success, and I'm sure my boss would sing my praises*
> *for my business and marketing initiative."*

3. *Don't send your cover letter as an attachment.*
Just write your cover letter as you would to any other email. That's what email is for. Your cover letter will

serve as the bait for the employer to open your resume.

4. *Respond with the title of the job advertisement in the subject heading.*
When you are sending your cover letter, write an email subject line that distinguishes you from others. Don't write a vague or generic one such as "Resume" or "Resume, EFG Inc." Make sure your subject line stands out among all the others by giving it unique and creative wording.

Yes, it's good to use some initiative in the subject line to grab attention.

> *Bad :* **Resume**
> *Good :* **Operations Manager (Telecommute)**
> *Best :* **Operations Manager (Telecommute) – I fit the bill!**

5. *Win them over by being open and honest.*
Be proud of your achievements, but a little modesty causes you to look human. It's good to know someone who admits they've failed, than someone who pretends they've always been successful.

> *"I successfully led a ten person team to generate sales of*
> *$200,000."*

Yeah, ok... but I'd respect that person even more if they had the balls to write this:

> *"In my last job, I had ten people working for me. It was stressful, and I didn't have a clue about how to manage at the time. Two of my team resigned in the first month, and I found it difficult to motivate the other eight who were all older than me. We still achieved our quota, but I was let go.*
>
> *To be fair, I was in over my head at the time. I have since been to two leadership training*

seminars, and I can see now where I went wrong."

But, don't be honestly stupid. Honesty, is not the best policy in some cases like this:

> *"Quite frankly, I've never used CMS and I don't even know*
> *what CMS stands for..."*

Either don't mention your lack of qualifications or spend ten minutes to go figure out what these applications do.

Final Thoughts on Email Cover Letters

When writing email cover letters, be sure to pay close attention to spelling, grammar, and tone, just as you would with a traditional cover letter. Perfection and accuracy are vital, as always.

The greatest advantage of email communications is immediacy. If you send cover letters and resumes online, you'll receive e-mail responses within a day or two, compared to a week or longer delay for responses to your mailed letters.

CHAPTER 5: **YOUR RESUME**

When writing a resume, many of you may know what you are meant to include. Your work history, educational background and other related experiences are essential to allowing your potential employer the opportunity to know your qualifications for the position and your potential with their organization. However, do you know what not to include in a resume? There are certain bits of information that should not be included.

Once you know the items that should be removed or deleted from your resume, you may find that it will be more appealing, more outlined and important information about you is easier to find. When employers are looking through resumes, they are looking for those that catch their attention. If all of your education and job experience is hidden by unnecessary information, they may skip over your application.

Two Types of Resumes

There are two primary formats that are used to create resumes. Either may be used depending upon the impact you'd like to make and what type of profession you are applying to.

1. **Skill Resume**

Recommended for those with a limited or sporadic work history, changing careers or those that have gained experience from sources other than direct employment in the field. Best for recent college graduates whose only paid work is in fast food chain and call center.

This resume format is a good example of how it can

help someone who does not have the best credentials. It allows the job seeker to present school and extracurricular activities to good effect. It is a strong format choice because it lets highlight strengths without emphasizing limited work experience.

Ana C. Perez
123 Lava Court • Denver, CO 81613
Home: (312) 393-1509
Cell: (313) 443-1352
ana.perez@gmail.com

Position Desired
Customer Service Representative in a retail sales or distribution business.

Skills and Abilities

Communications	Good written and verbal presentation skills. Use proper grammar and have a good speaking voice.
Interpersonal	Able to get along well with coworkers and accept supervision.
Skills	Received positive evaluations from previous supervisors.
Flexible	Willing to try new things and am interested in improving efficiency on assigned tasks.
Attention to Detail	Concerned with quality. Produce work that is orderly and attractive. Ensure tasks are completed correctly and on time.
Hardworking	Throughout high school, worked long hours in strenuous activities while attending school full-time.

Often managed as many as 65 hours a week |

	in school and other structured activities while maintaining above-average grades.
Customer Service	Routinely handled as many as 500 customer contacts a day (10,000 per month) in a busy retail outlet. Averaged lower than a .001% complaint rate and won the "Employee of the Month" award in second month of employment. Received two merit increases.
Cash Sales	Handled more than $2,000 a day ($40,000 a month) in cash sales. Balanced register and prepared daily sales summary and deposits. Reliable Excellent attendance record; trusted to deliver daily cash deposits totaling more than $40,000 a month.

Education

Franklin High School, 2007–2010. Classes included advanced English. Member of award-winning band. Excellent attendance record. Superior communication skills. Graduated in top 30% of class.

Other

Active gymnastics competitor for four years. Learned discipline, teamwork, how to follow instructions, and how to work hard. Ambitious, outgoing, and reliable, and have solid work ethic.

Note: It is essential that your resume emphasize the skills you have that directly support your ability to do the job you want.

2. **Chronological Resume.**
Probably the most commonly used format. This type

of resume presents your work experience and history in chronological order. By doing so, you can show your career growth, field and professional experience as it relates to the position you've applied for and can show employers your steady employment history.

A chronological resume is easy to develop, which gives this format a big advantage over other styles. The chronological format works best for those who have had several years of experience in the same type of job they are seeking now. This is because a chronological resume clearly displays your recent work experience.

Most employers find a chronological resume perfectly acceptable, as long as it is neat and has no errors.

Karen A. Ashton

115 South Hawthorne Avenue
kashton@yahoo.com
Chicago, IL 66204
(312) 653-5467(cell)

SUMMARY

Administrative professional with eight years of experience in private and public office settings, particularly in insurance and finance. Highly skilled in a variety of tasks, including office management, word processing, and spreadsheet and database program use.

EDUCATION AND TRAINING

Acme Business College, Lincoln, IL
Completed one-year program in Professional Office Management. Achieved GPA in top 30% of class. Courses included word processing, accounting theory and systems, advanced spreadsheet and database applications, graphics

design, time management, and supervision.

John Kennedy High School, South Bend, IN
Graduated with emphasis on business courses. Earned excellent grades in all business topics and won top award for word-processing speed and accuracy.

Other: Continuing-education programs at own expense, including business communications, customer relations, computer applications, and sales techniques.

EXPERIENCE

X-present—**Claims Processor, Red Tag Insurance Company**, Wilmette, IL
Process 50 complex medical insurance claims per day, almost 20% above department average. Created a spreadsheet report process that decreased
department labor costs by more than $30,000 a year. Received two merit raises for performance.

XXXX-XXXX—**Returned to business school to gain advanced office skills**.

XXXX-XXXX—**Finance Specialist (E4)**, U.S. Army
Systematically processed more than 200 invoices per day from commercial vendors. Trained and supervised eight employees. Devised internal system allowing 15% increase in invoices processed with a decrease in personnel. Managed department with a budget equivalent of more than $350,000 a year. Honorable discharge.

XXXX-XXXX—**Sales Associate promoted to Assistant Manager, Trisha's Boutique**, Wilmette, IL
Made direct sales and supervised four employees. Managed daily cash balances and deposits, made purchasing and inventory decisions, and handled all management functions during owner's absence. Sales increased 25% and profits doubled during tenure.

XXXX-XXXX—**Held various part-time and summer jobs through high school while maintaining GPA 3.0/4.0**. Earned enough to pay all personal expenses, including car insurance. Learned to deal with customers, meet deadlines, work hard, and handle multiple priorities.

> **STRENGTHS AND SKILLS**
> Reliable, with strong work ethic. Excellent interpersonal, written, and oral communication and math skills. Accept supervision well, effectively supervise others, and work well as a team member. General ledger, accounts payable, and accounts receivable expertise. Proficient in Microsoft Word, Excel, PowerPoint, and Outlook.

Note: In the past you might have seen a resume that included the word "Resume" at the top, just in case the reader didn't know what it was. But these days, everyone will know what it is, so that heading is not necessary.

Things Not To Include About Yourself

When applying for a job or career, it's important to understand that the characteristics you should be presenting are those that correspond with your history of performance and that personal traits and other information are not necessary and could result in discrimination. This is true specially when applying for an online job.

a. *Age*

Want it or not, some hiring managers will discriminate against employees based on their age. Technically, this form of discrimination is illegal, but if you seem too young or too old to do the job, you may not even get an interview - despite what the rest of the resume says

b. *Religion*

Going over religion in the workplace is an additional big no-no for Americans. Including your religion, or lack thereof, on a resume is too controversial and is irrelevant to the job. So unless you're applying for a job at a religious institution, exclude this information.

c. *Personal Hobbies*
Even though some employers like to see that interviewees are active in the community or have won non-professional awards, no one wishes to know that you love knitting with your grandmother. When in doubt, leave it out.

d. *Health Issues*
Money-Zine.com reports that "an employer has no legal right to know your health status. The only health-related questions that an employer can ask are job related." If you and your doctor feel that your health is adequate enough to complete your job duties as expected, then your health issues are no one else's business.

e. *Marital status or sexual orientation*
Your sexual preference does not have any significance on how well you can perform the job. Leave it out when writing up your resume, because reported by Emurse.com, "discrimination still exists in the hiring process, and [including this information] may lead to a premature and fully unwarranted disposal of your resume."

f. *Photograph*
JobFairy.com reports that hiring departments "legally cannot consider your picture in determining in case you are to be interviewed, or hired," and that "many companies won't even consider resumes that are submitted with a picture to make sure that they are in compliance with [the Equal Opportunity Employer]" legislation.

But, bear in mind, however, that if you are applying for jobs overseas, photographs may be the norm.

When sending photographs place it at the upper left hand corner of your resume. Do not send or attach a separate file with your picture.

g. *Physical Characteristics*
Just as you should never submit a photograph along with your resume, it's also best to leave out your physical characteristics, such as your height, weight and hair color, in writing. Describing yourself as a "hot blonde" is asking for trouble; conversely, overweight job seekers are sometimes unfairly discriminated against.

h. *Information About Your Family Members*
Whether or not you're married or have children does not belong on a resume. Some supervisors automatically assume that a parent of small children will be unavailable to work odd hours, but you should be the one to make that call, not them.

i. *Low GPAs*
Unless you're fresh out of college and looking for your first big job online, don't bother including your GPA. A good track record in your employment history will go much further in impressing the hiring department than a GPA that shows you got A's and B's in psychology eight years ago. This rule holds true especially if you had a low GPA in school.

Things Not To Include About Your History
Equally important to making certain your resume is looked upon with fair consideration is to ensure that it is not overlooked because it is too informative. When employers look through resumes, it is much like you are viewing a web page. You look for the highlights and bullet points to see if you'd like to read further. If your resume is jam-packed with insignificant information, it may be discarded. There is no need to include:

a. *Prior salary*

Although some employers request a salary history, you should not include it on your resume. Simply create that separate sheet and attach with your resume.

b. *High school education*
This is for those that have higher degrees and have completed college coursework.

c. *Irrelevant job experience*
Job experience that is unrelated to the position you're applying for only clutters your resume and irritates the HR department.

d. *References*
These do not need to be included in your resume. You can however make a small note at the end that states "References Available Upon Request"

But, if the job posts says so it's very important that you include it.

Note: When creating a resume, it's generally best to leave out overly personal information like your marital status, physical characteristics and any other attributes that could be controversial.

Bad grammar, typographical errors and formatting discrepancies does not belong on a resume. It shows that you are lazy, uneducated and don't care enough about the job to pay attention to detail. It's best to let someone else look over your resume as a precaution to make sure the hiring department can focus on your skills and experience — not your carelessness.

Important Notes When Sending Your Email Resume

When you're sending an email resume, it's advisable to follow the employer's instructions on how to submit your cover letter and resume. The employer may want your resume attached to the email message and sent in specific format, typically as a Microsoft Word document or a PDF.

When applying for employment via email, copy and paste your cover letter into the email message or write your cover letter in the body of an email message.

If the job posting asks you to send an attachment, send your resume as a PDF or a Word document. If you have word processing software other than Microsoft Word save your resume as a Word (.doc) document. *File*, *Save As*, should be an option in your program.

To save your document as a PDF, depending on your word processing software you may be able to File, Print to Adobe PDF. If not, there are programs you can use to convert file to a PDF.

Some employers do not accept attachments. In these cases, paste your resume into your email message as plain text. Use a simple font and remove the fancy formatting. Don't use HTML. You don't know what email client the employer is using, so, simple is best because the employer may not see a formatted message the same way you do.

Wrapping it Up: Do's and Dont's

- DO indicate what position you're applying for. Be specific, the company may be hiring for more than one job.

- DO tell them how to contact you. As the bare

minimum, leave your phone number and email address.

- DO highlight the skills and equipment you have that is suitable for telecommuting.

- DO send a cover letter with EVERY resume you send out!

- DO highlight all your computer skills, how fast you type, and what computer programs you are familiar with.

- DO use varied and detailed action verbs where necessary instead of relying simply on phrases such as "Responsible for." However, do not get overly creative and do not use excessively complicated words when simpler, more concise language will suffice. Remember that the best way make your resume stand out among the others is to be the most professional and easiest to read, rather than the one that looks the flashiest.

- DO study the job description or advertisement and try to incorporate the same keywords into your resume. If they use the word "adept in Microsoft Office applications..." use it "I'm adept in Microsoft Office applications...". This is very effective you're giving the employer an impression that you read and understand what was posted.

- DON'T misspell the hiring party wrong or substitute someone else's name.

- DON'T make spelling mistakes, typos, grammatical errors, and formatting problems like you wouldn't believe. One person said that her greatest strength was her attention to 'detal' (should have been DETAIL); another said it was his responsibility to 'a tent to customers' (ATTEND to customers).

- DON'T discuss the reasons WHY you want to work from home (I have kids, health problems...etc)

- DON'T use the phrase "work at home", use "telecommute from my home office" instead (more professional).

- DON'T mass mail, do not simply create a basic resume and send it to every job opening you find. A resume that seems basic and appears to be part of a mass-mailing has a much higher chance of being ignored and simply tossed in the recycling bin.

- DON'T put generic objectives your objective should be specific for the company and opening that you are applying for. In some specific cases, the objective may also be replaced with career or skill summaries if you feel that they may be beneficial.

- DON'T send a email to an employer asking if they are "legitimate" SEND YOUR cover letter and resume instead.

- DON'T be afraid to follow up with another letter 5 – 6 days after you send in your resume. Some were saying at least 1 - 2 weeks but I find it more effective to follow up after just a few days specially to those posted as URGENTLY Needed...

CHAPTER 6: **YOUR JOB INTERVIEW & SALARY NEGOTIATION**

I've read that job interviews are showbiz. Really.

When you're engaged in a selection interview, your entire future may rest on how successful you are in presenting yourself to a stranger.

Like reality shows on TV, interviews are based on reality but, in fact, are
staged. And as in reality shows, only one survivor beats the competition to win the prize.

The most successful interviews for you require solid preparation to learn
your lines, showing your future bosses that you're smart and quick on the
uptake, as well as able to communicate and not likely to jump the tracks.

At each meeting, your goal is to deliver a flawless performance that rolls off your tongue and gets the employer applauding — and remembering
you.

Perfect candidate, you!

Key Concepts That Can Make You A Star During The Job Interview:

1. **Plan ahead**
Preparation makes all the difference in whether you get the job as you face intense scrutiny and field probing questions. During the interview you must show that

you're tuned in to the company's needs, that you have the skills to get up to speed quickly, and that you're the best fit with the company.

2.Connect all your qualifications with a job's requirements

If a quick glance at your notes reminds you that the interviewer missed a
requirement or two listed in the job posting when describing the position's scope and the ideal person for it, help the interviewer by tactfully bringing up the missing criteria yourself. Keep it simple:

> *I see from my notes that your posting asked for five years of experience. I have that and two years more, each with a record of solid performance in . . ..*

You want to demonstrate that you take this job possibility seriously, an
attitude that the employer will applaud.

3. Memorize short-form sales statements about yourself

Almost certainly, you will be asked to respond to some version of the "tell me about yourself" question. You're not helping your hiring chances if your respond is like this: *"My name is Jane Doe. I'm 28 years old. We are 8 in the family and I'm the eldest. My hobbies are writing, reading and watching TV..."* Don't laugh that happens and I've heard a lot of that responses when I'm interviewing people for telemarketer's position. This approach makes you sound silly and unprepared.

Instead, commit to memory a short-form sales statement (two minutes max, and preferably less than one minute) that describes your education, experience, and skills, and matches your strengths to the jobs you seek.

Your goal is to impress the hiring manager by telling your "story" in about 20 to 30 seconds, or in 100 words or less:

After I graduated from ABC University, I worked in the insurance industry until I took a break to start a family. That accomplished, I went back for refresher education. Now, thoroughly updated, I'm looking for a new connection in either the insurance or financial fields.

4. **Be likeable**

Likeability is a huge factor in choosing and keeping employees. Given a choice of technically qualified applicants, employers almost always choose the one they like best. For your purposes, remember this:

We like people who are like us.

Everyone likes to work with agreeable, sunny people. People rarely hire someone they don't like.

5. **Remember that you have a speaking part**

Communication skills are among the most desired qualities employers say they want. Answer questions clearly and completely. Be sure to observe all social skills of conversation — no interrupting, no profanity. Just as you shouldn't limit yourself to one or two-word answers, neither should you try to cover your nervousness with surround-sound endless talking. Aim for a happy medium.

Steer clear of negative words (such as *hate, don't ever want, absolutely not*, and *refuse*).

And remember, don't just sell, sell, sell. Take time to listen. When you're constantly busy thinking of what you're going to say next, you miss vital points and openings.

So work on your listening skills. When you don't understand an interviewer's question, ask for clarification.

21st-Century Video Interview

The 21st-century transition of the job interviewing process to video screens one that's evolving minute by minute — adds a whole new layer of techniques you'll want to master for successful job hunting.

This section will describe the essentials of nailing the video interview through Skype.

Skype is an online phone and video Internet service. But you need a computer, a webcam, and a decent broadband connection.

Before you make your first screen appearance on the interview scene via
video chat on Skype, take the following steps:

- Download the Skype software a week or two in advance.
- Create a professional username; this isn't the scene to joke around.

How To Handle A Job Interview Over Skype

More companies are tapping into Skype and other video communication tools to interview job seekers.

Speaking with a prospective employer over an Internet connection is not without stumbling blocks.

Here are some tips to help you do it right.

1. Dress the part, even if you're sitting in your living room, wear what you'd wear in a face to face interview not your every day shirt.

Do not do the interview in your room it will make you look very unprofessional and it might send other message to your prospective employer.

2. Check your lighting. Make sure your face is well lit up.

3. Clean up. You want the space around you to look tidy. Get rid of that pile of dirty laundry and avoid distractions. Clear out all that clutter.

4. Frame yourself. Adjust your computer's camera so that it points directly at your face not off to the side.

5. Do a test call with your mother, brother or friend. Check the sound and light. A test run will help make sure things go smoothly in the interview.

6. During the interview avoid distractions. Make sure your family know that you'll need quiet and can't be interrupted. If you have pets make sure they're not in the room.

7. Turn your cellphones off and close any other application on your computer. You don't want to receive texts, emails or phone calls during the interview. They could make you look distracted and unfocused.

8. Look at the camera not your computer screen. The only way the interviewer can see your eyes is through the camera lens. Looking down at the screen shifts your eyes downward and makes it look like you're not paying attention. So keep your eyes on the camera's lens. It's the only way interviewers can establish a connection with you.

9. Don't fidget, video software has a delay of a few seconds making your gestures look blurry. If you talk with your hands try sitting on them.

10. Be prepared for tech problems. Address any technical issues upfront, before the interview

gets underway. Ask who will call back if the connection drops. And if a video delay missed a question ask your
interviewer to repeat it.

Virtual Handshake

Unless your interview space is on fire, it's not your prerogative to end the interview. Always allow the interviewer to indicate when time's up. Since at the end of a video interview you can't shake hands through a monitor, deliver a sign-off statement indicating you understand that the interview is over. You can say something as simple as *"Thank you for interviewing me. I enjoyed it. Let's talk again soon."*

> ***Note:*** The three most important things to remember in a video interview are (1) smile, (2) smile, and (3) smile. Have you noticed that, even when reporting disasters of nationwide proportions, TV anchor people don't always wipe the smile off their faces? Why do you suppose that is? Smile!

Salary Negotiation

Do you know why most of the times the salary questions come early during the interview?

The salary question comes up quickly when the interviewer:

- Is trying to instantly determine your professional level, or is slyly probing to see whether you'll be happy with the low side of an offer.
- Wants to test the market. The interviewer may not even have an idea of the position's market value and is shopping candidates to simplify budgeting.

- Is open to paying whatever is necessary to get the right person and just wants to know what he's in for.

Whatever the interviewer's motivation for prying a salary disclosure from you, without a job offer, salary disclosures put too much power in the employer's hands.

Money Talk with Smart Replies
This section gives you a number of script lines to use in response to premature questions about your salary expectations.

Don't let a frog clog your throat when an interviewer presses for the salary discussion before you've established your value. Instead, answer along the following lines:

I'm sure that money won't be a problem after I'm able to show you how my qualifications can work to your advantage because they closely match your requirements.

I'm aware of the general range for my kind of work, but I'd feel better talking about pay once we've established what specific performance goals the job calls for.

I'd be kidding if I said money isn't important to me — sure, it is! But the job itself and the work environment are also very important to me. I wonder if we can hold the pay issue for a bit?

I'm a great believer in matching pay with performance, so I can't speak with any certainty about the kind of money I'm looking for until I know more about what you need.

45

Money is not my only priority; I'd really like to discuss my contributions to the company first — if that's okay with you.

I can't answer that question until I know more about this job. The amount of my starting compensation is not as much of an issue to me as how satisfying my filling the position will be for both of us. Can we talk more about what the position entails?
Before we get into the compensation issue, can you tell me more about the kind of skills and the type of individual you're looking for to help you reach your goals? What do you expect the person you hire to accomplish within the first three months?

All I need is fair market value for the job's demands, which I'm sure you'll pay, so is it okay if we talk about the details of the job first?

As far as I can tell, the position seems like a perfect fit for me — tit for tat on your requirements and my qualifications. So as long as you pay in the industry ballpark, I'm sure that we won't have a problem coming up with a figure we're both happy with.

Before we can come to an agreement, I need to know more about your strategy for compensation, as well as confirm my understanding of the results you're looking for. Can we hold that question for a bit?

Since pay includes so many possibilities for compensation, I'd like to first know more about your compensation plan overall and how it relates to the position.

I'm sure that you have a fair salary structure, and if I'm the best candidate for the position, we can work something out that we'll all like.

I'm not used to talking money before a job offer; are you making me an offer? I will consider any reasonable offer. Should we talk about it after we've wrapped up the details of the job, and I've been able to show you what I bring to your company?

Try not to talk money until you know they want you.

Note: Suppose things are going positively for you, whether after the first or second interview, if you like them and you have a feeling that they like you too, a job offer will be made. Then and only then that, it is time to discuss the salary.

CHAPTER 7: **THE PSYCHOLOGY OF SCAMMING**

Scammers can be successful coning you because:

- You think it's a great deal.
- You don't look close enough (or want to look close enough) to see the fraud.
- You're desperate and you think they're your only option

We want to believe it's true because we need the job, we need the money, and we need the freedom of working from home. We prefer to believe, and so we forget about parts of the ad or post or websites that trigger the red flags to take away our belief.

Just about any great scammer will tell you that lies are most effective when there's a hint that there's truth in them.

Many scam ads out there will rely on this element of your psyche to lure you in.

Through out the ad you might see:

- Something you are aware of to be true.
- Something that is easy to assume to be true.
- Something that you're familiar with.
- Compelling beliefs that other people have had success.

Your logical mind may choose to take a backseat in this scenario because your emotional mind sees the part that is the truth, sees the part that you assumed true, and assumes that the part that you're not familiar with is also true. Couple that with compelling stories from other people who have had success and you're ready to fall for the scam.

How Not To Get Scammed Online

Many people have being scammed in the popular classified sites like the very popular Craiglist.org.

Let me share with you my experience in Craigslist.

Way back 2008 I sent an email application posted in Craigslist a few days after I received an email saying that they think I have the skills they're looking for. At first it seemed legitimate. The hiring manager sent me instructions and tests. I did them because they were exercises dealing with administration, which I am very familiar and experienced. A few days later he told me I passed all the exams and I'm finally hired but before I start working I need a kit that has all the training materials and software I can use to perform my daily tasks, the kit costs $200. I would bite in exchange of $1,800 pay every month but I don't have $200 that time so I passed and later on I read from a forum that he was a scam.

Now here's some things that you need to keep in mind to avoid situations like mine:

Check out the job listings . If it isn't listed in the job posting, find out if there's a salary or if you're paid on commission. For work at home jobs, ask how often are you paid and how you are paid. Ask what equipment (hardware/software) you need to provide.

You won't get rich quick (yeah really). Avoid listings that guarantee you wealth, financial success, or that will help you get rich fast. Stay clear of listings that offer you high income for part-time hours. They will do none of the above.

Check if the company website is legitimate
If you're not sure whether a site is legit, google it and see what information or reviews the results show, see what people are saying about the site and what experienced other people had with the site.

You can also check the Whois.com and Alexa.com which tells you all the information about the website from the date it was registered to the person that registered the site, the address and a lot more.

Check references
Ask for references if you're not sure about the company's legitimacy. Request a list of other employees or contractors to find out how this has worked for them. Then contact the references to ask how this is working out. If the company isn't willing to provide references (names, email addresses and phone numbers) do not consider the opportunity.

Get the names and email addresses, skype or yahoo of your co-workers. Ask them questions like if the employer give salary online etc.

If they give phone numbers, try to ring it just to check if a live person will answer.
 Carefully investigate companies that you are interested in.

In general, if a job says that you can earn a lot of money in a hurry with experience or skills necessary, the chances are good that it's not going to happen. The same holds true if there are fees for information, kits, or anything else. All of those are warning signs to watch for when job searching.

Typical Job Scam Examples

Bogus job

After you respond to a job posting via email, you are asked to fill out a form on another page in order to prove that you are not spamming them. That site is typically a pitch for a marketing or work at home scheme or a site selling something.

> *Note:* A warning sign is having to click on another site and submit information, rather than being able to apply for the job.

We made an error

You're told you have been hired and will be paid a weekly salary for an online marketing job. Then, the company sends another email saying that there was a mistake and they had accidentally sent four times the amount of your paycheck. You're told to wire the rest of the money to someone else when you receive the check.

> *Note:* These types of scams are a way to get you to send money to a third party. The check they send will bounce and you'll be out the amount you wired. In some cases, there will also be an attempt to get your bank account information.

Bank of ABC Earns $100 a Day

Example:

"Seeking a temporary currency supporter since I`m unavailable visiting relatives in France. It´s a quite simple job. I´m able to transfer upfront, daily amounts $1000. All you have to do is withdraw and send to one of our exchangers. Remember that you get to keep 10% for yourself, regardless of any fees. If you are wondering why I can´t do it myself, it is simply due to my current unavailability."

Note: These types of scams are usually either money laundering or a way to attempt to get your bank account information.

Various job titles

Example:

"Supply company currently needing persons for the following positions: Sales, Customer Service, Office Administration, Management opportunities for those who qualify. No experience needed, training provided. $400 - $1000 weekly. Only 10 positions left. Hurry, call now!"

Note: Positions like this are listed on multiple job sites with various job titles include sales, customer service, office position, etc. There is no company name, web address, location, or anything else other than a phone number.

Part Time / Full Time

Example:

"Earn $100 or $10K or more a month. Easy work from home position."

Note: You can find ads like this almost everywhere, this ad had a disclaimer in a tiny font at the bottom of the page which said there is risk involved and you might not do as well. Most of them don't even say that.

Managers Needed

Example:
"We are seeking individuals who really are ready to change their lives, join an award winning team, and work consistently part time or full time with me to become independently wealthy in the next 12 months. No experience necessary. Will train."

Note: When contacted the company attempts to sell a kit to get you started, which is a typical employment scam.

Unsolicited email job posting

Example:
"This email job posting offers a work at home part time position as a Regional Manager. The job includes processing payments between the partners' clients and the company."

Note: This job posting was full of red flags. It was an unsolicited email message - I hadn't applied for the job or posted my resume. The message wasn't addressed to me and the return address was a personal email address, not a company one. When I search in google the company name the top results were all on scam warning sites. In addition, processing payments is another typical scam designed to collect your bank account information.

Work at Home Jobs To Avoid

- **Data entry jobs** - You'll see lots of listings for data entry jobs. They are usually either positions posting ads or a sales pitch for a kit that will get you started.

- **Packing jobs** - No, you can't make lots of money packing craft kits or any other type of kits. You can waste money on a package to get you started though.

- **Multi-Level Marketing (MLM)** - Which involves recruiting new people, and more new people, to sell the product. If all you are doing is trying to find more people to do what you're doing, keep in mind that there are probably thousands of other people attempting to do the same thing. Most of them aren't getting rich. Also note, that MLM isn't a job with a paycheck - it's starting a business, with no guarantees.

- **Posting Ads** - There are lots of ads saying workers are needed to post ads on online bulletin boards and forums. You don't get paid to post, rather you may get paid if other people sign-up.

- **Processing claims** - In order to get "hired" you'll need to buy equipment, software and pay for training.

- **Stuffing envelopes** - Believe it or not, there are still people saying that you can earn $3 or $4 per envelope to stuff them. You can't. All major companies have postage machines which stuff, sort and meter mail.

Where To Report Scams

If you been scammed online there are plenty of places to report it, like the ripoffreport.com and the ice3.org which is a government branch only for online scams and online security, there are plenty more but if you get scammed don't sit back your testimonial could help someone else from falling in the same scam. Report the company to the Better Business Bureau (BBB). Enter the company name or the web site into the Better Business Bureau search box to find out whether there have been complaints and whether the company has an unsatisfactory record with the Bureau. You can file your own complaint online.

What am I doing wrong? - I've applied for so many jobs and am not hearing back from anyone.

It's important to remember that there's a lot of competition for legitimate home-based work, so it may take awhile to land the job or project you want. Also, many employers have done away with the "formalities" of acknowledging receipt of an application, and no longer notify all applicants when a position has been filled.

You can improve your chances by making sure you have a stand out cover letter and resume – one that focuses on what you can do for the company.

You should also highlight your ability to work independently, your familiarity with virtual communications tools (e.g., instant messenger, Skype, GoToMyPC, or others), and, where appropriate, your home-based work experience.

If you don't have a blog, consider starting one, to show your understanding of online communications, and to demonstrate your expertise in your specialty or niche. I recommend Wordpress.com, Tumblr and Blogger I tried using them and they're all excellent specially for beginners. (It's free, as well.)

Also, be sure to follow instructions exactly. If the job lead requests a resume in the body of an email, DO NOT attach your resume – paste your resume in text format into an email (more on that below), and send it directly to the party or email address specified in the lead.

If the job lead specifies a written reply (online application form, resume, etc.), DO NOT phone the company to express an interest or request additional information. Human Resources personnel list this among their chief complaints, and smaller hirers may resent the interruption even more.

Failure to follow directions at the time of application is also often viewed as an inability or unwillingness to follow directions in general – not a trait most employers are seeking.

GUIDE CHECKLIST AND WORKBOOK

DAY 1

From Chapter 1 I said that necessary to job and career satisfaction specially if you are going to work-from-home is matching your own unique talents, skills, and interests, and personality to those job related task and activities that you find most enjoyable, interesting, and challenging to do.

Today you are provided with questions that can help you assess your self to find the right work-from-home career.

Begin self-assessment:

1. List down the things that you can you do and the things that you are good at?

_____

_____

_____

2. List down the things that you want to do.

_____

_____

_____

3. Describe the kind of people you want to work with.

_____

_____

_____

4. Write down things you think you are better at than other people.

_____

_____

_____

5. Write down any particular things that are important to you, and things that "you won't budge from."

_____

_____

DAY 2

Review your answers to your self-assessment.

Today, we are going to create a free account at Guru.com and explore the freelance market place.

Let's get started.

Explore Guru.com

> **Step 1:** Visit http://www.guru.com/ and click on the "Freelancers: Looking for work?"

> **Step 2:** Click the (1) category and the (2) sub-category that matches your desired job.

> **Step 3:** Next you will see all Projects/Jobs posted by employers. The page will show you the (1) most recent job posted, (2) when the posting will expire, (3) number of proposals already submitted, (4) number of invited job seekers that has account in guru.com, (5) short description of skills required for the job, (6) budget alloted for the position, (7) the employers total money spent, (8) feedback received.

> **Step 4:** Click the job title to view job description read more about those that catch your interest. Repeat the process searching through other categories.

> **Step 5:** Write down ten interesting and popular jobs you uncovered and make a note of these jobs. Make sure you list only the job that fits the job that you are

looking for based on the job description.

Job Link	Job Title Job	Rate
e.g. http://www.guru.com/pro/proje ctdetail.aspxProjectId=710977 &ItemNo=11&SearchUrl=sear ch.aspx?	Native English - Virtual Assistant!	8
_____	_____	_____
_____	_____	_____
_____	_____	_____
_____	_____	_____
_____	_____	_____
_____	_____	_____
_____	_____	_____

Creating Your Free Account at Guru.com

1. Click the "Register" link located above the menu bar.

2. Be sure to select the "Create a Freelance Account (Get Work)" tab. Complete the required information. Click the Submit button at the bottom of the page once you've double-checked your information and

agreed to the terms:

3. After registering a Freelancer account, you must post at least one profile so Employers can view your skills and the services you offer. Your profile will also enable you to search for and submit proposals on projects, and it will be matched with new project postings.

Explore Guru.com and make yourself comfortable with the interface.

DAY 3

Today we will explore Craigslist.

Craigslist.org is among the most effective and free sites on the internet used to find pretty much everything. Buy, sell, and is a very useful source of job listings in a specific location. Jobs are listed by location and category. You can also post your resume to your local Craigslist site.

Let's start.

Step 1: Go to Craigslist http://www.craigslist.org

Step 2: Select the City or State from which you are located.

The simpliest way to find jobs on Craigslist is to go to the city or state site where you are interested in looking for jobs. You'll see a directory of sites on the right side of the original Craigslist page or you can go directly to the list of Craigslist - Cities. Not all cities have a dedicated site, so if you don't see your city, use the state site.

Step 3: Once you've reached the location you want, either click on the type of job or click on "Jobs" to run a keyword search.

Step 4: Click the job postings that interests you. Instructions on how to apply are included in the individual job posting.

Repeat the process searching through other job categories.

Step 5: Like what you did in Day 2 for Guru.com write down ten popular jobs you find interesting and make a note of each, use the form below. And again make sure you list only the job that fits the job that you are looking for based on the job description.

Step 6: Resume Posting. You'll find a link that says "Resumes" at the bottom of the list of job listing categories. Click on it and you'll be able to upload your resume.

Job Link	Job Title Job	Rate
e.g. http://www.guru.com/pro/proje ctdetail.aspxProjectId=710977 &ItemNo=11&SearchUrl=sear ch.aspx?	Native English - Virtual Assistant!	8
_____	_____	_____
_____	_____	_____
_____	_____	_____
_____	_____	_____
_____	_____	_____
_____	_____	_____

Most people I know grumble that they never get hired on Craigslist. If you wish to get hired, you need to stand out with your work and application. Create amazing resume and cover letter and send a portfolio to show off your talent.

Since you have explored and created account to some freelance job sites go to one or more of the following top job boards and job search engine sites filled with thousands of work-from-home opportunities.

LinkUp http://www.linkup.com

SimplyHired http://www.simplyhired.com

Monster http://www.monster.com

CareerBuilder.com
http://www.careerbuilder.com

Indeed http://www.indeed.com

Fiverr http://fiverr.com

Backpage http://www.backpage.com

Elance.com http://www.elance.com

SoloGig http://www.sologig.com

ClicknWork http://clicknwork.com

Ether http://www.ether.com

Day 04

Now, that you have discovered the most popular job sites you are now ready to send your resume and cover letter.

Use the checklist to make sure you have included all relevant information in your resume. Always personalize and customize your resume, so, it reflects your skills and abilities and connects them with the jobs you are applying for.

Resume Checklist:

Presentation and Layout	Yes	No
Is my resume laid out and presented in a professional manner?		
Are my headings and sub-headings clear?		
Did I make sure that my headings, fonts, dates and titles are consistent?		
Did I use indentation, underlining, capitals, and white space effectively?		
Did I organize my resume in a logical manner?		
Language	**Yes**	**No**

	Yes	No
Is my language usage clear and straight forward?		
Did I make sure that my sentences begin with an *action verb whenever possible? (*Action Verb:* Use the list below of action verb examples to assist you in writing your resume.)		
Did I use key words and phrases that are relevant to my target work area?		
Did I double-check that my grammar, punctuation and spelling are all correct?		
Did I write in the past tense for events that happened in the past and the present tense for present events?		
Did I remember to avoid using jargon and abbreviations?		
Overall	**Yes**	**No**
Is my resume tailored to the specific position I'm applying for?		
Did I provide only truthful information?		

Action Verbs *

Communication People Skills

Addressed	Conveyed	Formulated	Moderated
Advertised	Convinced	Furnished	Negotiated
Arbitrated	Corresponded	Incorporated	Observed
Arranged	Debated	Influenced	Outlined
Articulated	Defined	Interacted	Participated
Authored	Developed	Interpreted	Persuaded
Clarified	Directed	Interviewed	Presented
Collaborated	Discussed	Involved	Promoted
Communicated	Drafted	Joined	Proposed
Composed	Edited	Judged	Publicized
Condensed	Elicited	Lectured	Reconciled
Conferred	Enlisted	Listened	Recruited
Consulted	Explained	Marketed	Referred
Contacted	Expressed	Mediated	Reinforced

Creative Skills

Acted	Created	Established	Introduced
Adapted	Customized	Fashioned	Invented

Began	Designed	Formulated	Modeled
Cared for	Developed	Founded	Modified
Combined	Directed	Illustrated	Originated
Composed	Displayed	Initiated	Performed
Conceptualized	Drew	Instituted	Photographed
Condensed	Entertained	Integrated	Planned

Data / Financial Skills

Analyzed	Determined	Formulated	Located
Clarified	Diagnosed	Gathered	Measured
Collected	Evaluated	Identified	Organized
Compared	Examined	Inspected	Researched
Conducted	Experimented	Interviewed	Reviewed
Critiqued	Explored	Invented	Searched
Detected	Extracted	Investigated	Solved

Helping Skills

Adapted	Clarified	Educated	Helped
Advocated	Coached	Encouraged	Insured
Aided	Collaborated	Ensured	Intervened
Answered	Contributed	Expedited	Mentored
Arranged	Cooperated	Facilitated	Motivated

Assessed	Counseled	Familiarized	Prevented
Assisted	Demonstrated	Furthered	Provided
Cared for	Diagnosed	Guided	Referred

Management / Leadership Skills

Administered	Coordinated	Headed	Navigated
Analyzed	Decided	Hired	Organized
Appointed	Delegated	Hosted	Originated
Approved	Developed	Improved	Overhauled
Assigned	Directed	Increased	Oversaw
Attained	Eliminated	Initiated	Planned
Authorized	Emphasized	Inspected	Presided
Chaired	Enforced	Instituted	Prioritized
Considered	Enhanced	Led	Produced
Consolidated	Established	Managed	Recommended
Contracted	Executed	Merged	Reorganized
Controlled	Generated	Motivated	Replaced
Converted	Handled		Restored

Organizational Skills

Approved	Corresponded	Monitored	Registered
Arranged	Distributed	Obtained	Reserved

Catalogued	Executed	Operated	Responded
Categorized	Filed	Ordered	Reviewed
Charted	Generated	Organized	Routed
Classified	Implemented	Prepared	Scheduled
Coded	Incorporated	Processed	Screened
Collected	Inspected	Provided	Set up
Compiled	Logged	Purchased	Sorted
Corrected	Maintained	Recorded	Submitted

Research Skills

Analyzed	Determined	Formulated	Located
Clarified	Diagnosed	Gathered	Measured
Collected	Evaluated	Identified	Organized
Compared	Examined	Inspected	Researched
Conducted	Experimented	Interviewed	Reviewed
Critiqued	Explored	Invented	Searched
Detected	Extracted	Investigated	Solved

Teaching Skills

Adapted	Critiqued	Focused	Persuaded
Advised	Developed	Guided	Set goals
Clarified	Enabled	Individualized	Simulated

Coached	Encouraged	Informed	Stimulated
Communicated	Evaluated	Instilled	Taught
Conducted	Explained	Instructed	Tested
Coordinated	Facilitated	Motivated	Trained

Technical Skills

Adapted	Constructed	Fabricated	Programmed
Applied	Converted	Fortified	Rectified
Assembled	Debugged	Installed	Regulated
Built	Designed	Maintained	Remodeled
Calculated	Determined	Operated	Repaired
Computed	Developed	Overhauled	Replaced
Conserved	Engineered	Printed	Restored

More Skills

Achieved	Electrified	Perfected	Spearheaded
Completed	Expanded	Quoted	Transferred
Effected	Pioneered	Sparked	Treated

* Action Verbs information adapted from the following sources:

- http://www.quintcareers.com/action_skills.html

- http://www.asu.edu/studentaffairs/career/Files/

ActionVerbs.pdf

After checking and rechecking your resume next step is to review your cover letter to make sure that you have covered all the basics and are sending a perfect cover letter to your prospective employer.

Cover Letter Checklist

Overall Presentation	Yes	No
Is the contact name and company name correct?		
Did I addressed the letter to an individual, (if the job post mentioned the name of the individual.)?		
Did the letter mention where I saw the job posting?		
Is my cover letter targeted to the position I'm applying for?		
Font is 10 or 12 points and easy to read (Times New Roman or Arial, for example).		
There are no spelling, grammatical or typographical errors.		
Did I read the cover letter out loud to make sure there are no missing words?		
Did I proofread my cover letter?		

Day 05

Review the lessons and suggestions of your main guide book. Today we will check which of your web presence will hurt our online application.

What Employers Can Find About You Online

 When you're job searching, consider your personal information that can easily be found online by potential employers. Based on Susan Heathfield's Employer Survey, almost 50% say they check candidates at Google or another search engine. Given that many employers really do research job applicants, it's important to ensure that all your communications are professional.

The many communications that can tell employers a lot about you include email, instant message, blogs, and the content and photos you post on social networking sites like Facebook, and Twitter.

Take the time to periodically check all the information you have (or someone else has about you) online, so you can make sure you don't get any unpleasant surprises during the hiring process.

Here's a quick list of what you should check.

Email / Instant Message (IM)	Yes	No
Are your email address and instant messenger screen name(s) are professional?		
Does your email messages include a signature with your phone number, so, it's easy for employers to contact you. *(One way to avoid mixing business with pleasure is to have a dedicated email address and screen name that you use just for job searching.)*		
Google	**Yes**	**No**
Have you Googled yourself to see what information people can find about you on the Internet? *(Make sure that what you find is appropriate for a potential employer to read. You might be surprised at what's there!)*		
Blogs	**Yes**	**No**
Have you reviewed your personal information? *(If you blog or you have friends who write about you, check to make sure what they are writing is appropriate because any potential employer could find it.)*		
Social Networking	**Yes**	**No**

Check your twitter or facebook. Is there anything you wouldn't want a potential employer to see? *(If you're concerned, make your profile private and be careful what you put on the front page.)*		

It's important to protect your privacy when job searching online.

Even though you should be able to have a personal life online, employers want to find out as much about as candidates for employment as they can. There are ethical issues regarding how deeply employers should look for information, but, there's nothing stopping them from getting as much information as much as they can on you. So, be careful what you share - you're not just sharing it with your friends, you're sharing it with the world.

DAY 06

Before heading to your interview, go through this checklist to ensure you are prepared. Once you are confident with each item, you are ready.

Good luck!

Knowledge About the Company	Yes	No
Mission, Philosophy, Values		
Industry information		
Leadership position in the industry		
Organization's history		
Executive / Management Team		
Flagship products & services		
Competitors		
Markets (including opportunities and constraints)		
Any particular challenges / issues / accomplishments		
Any recent newsworthy items		

Know About the Job	Yes	No
Job Title and Description		
Knowledge, Skills, Abilities required		
Experience required		
Qualities required to be successful		
Ballpark compensation range (do your research!)		
Know your subject matter and terminology		
Any other details you can get through a contact inside the company, or others, including whether or not this is a new job, filling a vacant position, amount of travel, etc. – to avoid surprises and be able to tailor your points and responses accordingly		

Know Yourself	Yes	No
Your strengths		
Your weaknesses		
Your nature ("qualities")		
How you will improve in areas of challenge		
Your career goals		

The kind of organization you would thrive in		

Make Sure to Practice:	Yes	No
Basic questions (see Sample of Basic Questions below)		
Tricky and Off-the-Wall questions		
Turning negatives into positives		
Being brief!		
Your 5-minute life story		
Discussing items on your resume		

Make Sure to Have :	Yes	No
Interview time, date.		
Interviewer name(s), job title(s), role/responsibilities (if possible)		
Agenda or other calendar device to note dates pertaining to "next action'" items (such as when to call back, when you are available for another interview)		

Sample of Basic Questions:

1. What do you know about this company?

2. Tell me about yourself.

3. Why are you applying for this job

4. How would you describe yourself?

5. What are your major strengths?

6. What is your greatest weakness?

7. What type of work do you like to do best?

8. What are your interests outside of work?

9. What accomplishment gave you the greatest satisfaction?

10. Why did you leave your last job?

11. Why were you fired (if you were)?

12. Where do you see yourself 5 years from now?

13. What are your goals in life?

14. How much did you make at your last job?

The list goes on and on. But according to Richard Nelson Bolles author of What Color is Your Parachute. Beneath the dozens and dozens of possible questions that the employer could ask you, there are only five basic questions you need to pay attention to.

Five, just five. The people-who-have-the-power-to-hire-you usually wants to know the answers to these five questions, which they may ask directly or try to find out themselves:

1. **Why are you here?** They mean by this, "Why are you knocking on my door, rather than someone else's door?"

2. **What can you do for us?** They mean by this, "If I were to hire you, would you be part of the problems I already have, or would you be part of the solution to those problems? What are your skills, and how much do you know about some subject or field that is of interest to us?"

3. **What kind of person are you?** They mean by this, "Do you have the kind of personality that makes it easy for people to work with you, and do you share the values that we have at this place?"

4. **What distinguishes you from nineteen other people who can do the same tasks that you can?** They mean by this, "Do you have better work habits than the nineteen others, do you show up earlier, stay later, work more thoroughly, work faster, maintain higher standards, go the extra mile, or... what?"

5. **Can I afford you?** They mean by this, "If we decide we want you here, how much will it take to get you, and are we willing and able to pay that amount--- governed as we are, by our budget, and by our inability to pay you as much as the person who would be above you, on the organizational chart? "

These are the five principal questions that most employers are dying to know the answers to. Anything you can do, during the interview, to help the employer find the answers to these five questions, will make the interview very satisfying to the employer.

Day 07

Review Chapter 7 of your main guide book. Today we will go over with job scam warning signs checklist

.

Dear Applicant,

This is your prospective employer. Please send us your credit card details to process your application.

Sincerely,

Your soon-to-be-employer

Avoid falling victim to a work at home scam by recognizing the following warning signs in job advertisements:

Recognizing a Work at Home Scam	Yes	No
• Boasts no experience necessary		
• Promises easy money and huge part-time earnings		
• Promotes having "inside" business information		

• Asks you to purchase products or instructions before getting "hired"		
• No company name, web address, location, or anything else other than a phone number.		

Be careful and thoroughly investigate any job opening you find on any job sites before you apply. There are many different types of job scams and it's important to be careful to not be taken advantage of.

Good Luck on your Job Hunting!!!

ABOUT THE AUTHOR

Joy D. Gurtiza is a work-at-home mother with four children. She works for a Canadian marketing company as a Chief Operations Officer.

She has been working from home for more than 8 years and handled various jobs in managerial/leadership jobs but started as customer service, data entry, telemarketer, article writer, and virtual assistant.

After over 8 years of trial and error she has finally found ways to share all her hard-learned lessons, help others make a cover letter and resume that rocks the prospective employer. Identify scams and find legitimate work-at-home.

Joy is also a good cook and a food photographer. She keeps a food blog here: http://joybites.com.

www.ingramcontent.com/pod-product-compliance
Lightning Source LLC
Chambersburg PA
CBHW031302280526
45784CB00004B/1954